Employee Representative Guide
For non-union workplaces

Cilinnie Ngo-Pondi

ISBN-13: 978-1507861738
ISBN-10: 1507861737

DISCLAIMER

CONTENTS

1 INTRODUCTION

An Employee representative is an employee who speaks officially for an employee or group of employees and represents them in employer forums such as managers meetings, disciplinary proceedings, redundancy situations and transfers of undertakings. Employee Representatives are divided into Union Representatives and Non-union Representatives. This book is about employee representatives in a non-unionized workplace.

The legal framework governing employee representatives is quite complicated. There are at least 15 different pieces of legislation which lay down different rights for employee representatives, as well as Codes of Practice produced by ACAS and the Health & Safety Executive.

Union representatives are appointed by an independent union in workplaces where that union is recognised for collective bargaining purposes. They can include specialist representatives for union learning, health and safety, equality and diversity, information and consultation, pensions and many more.

They have more rights in the workplace than non-union employee representatives. This book aims to guide you in negotiating rights and facilities equivalent to the statutory rights given to union representatives.

In a non-union workplace, employee representatives are the only means through which employees can have a say in workplace matters that affect them.

According to ACAS[1], *"…..the role of Employee Representatives in non-unionized workplaces tends to be much more restricted than that of union counterparts, being limited in the main to consultation. In some cases, for example in dealing with collective redundancies and the transfer of undertakings in firms which do not recognise trade unions, non-union representatives have statutory rights to facilities, time off for training and facility time.*

For some other non-union representatives, especially members of consultative forums set up under the information and consultation regulations, and multinational companies with a European Works Council, the statutory provisions are only for time off with pay to carry out representative duties.

Often consultative bodies, usually called employee forums or works councils, are set up voluntarily by employers with no reference to the law. Here there are no enforceable rights to paid time off, training or the use of facilities."

In such a workplace, there is no general right or requirement to have employee representatives. European Union directives have affected the status of employee representatives and representative bodies by providing legal minimums which the UK must comply with. Employee representatives must be informed and consulted on collective redundancies, business transfers, health and safety, working time, pension scheme changes and proposed takeovers.

Larger employers may also need to set up European Works Councils or other information and consultation bodies to enable them to consult with UK or Europe-wide workforces about economic and employment-related matters affecting the business. European Companies (Societas Europaea) must set up employee involvement arrangements to enable employee representatives to participate in their decision-making processes.

A European Company cannot be registered until an employee involvement arrangement has been made. Any existing employee participation arrangements must be protected where a UK company merges with a company registered elsewhere in the European Union. A Court will not give approval for the merger unless arrangements for employee participation in the merged company have been agreed.

UK law implements these directives through regulations requiring employers to inform and consult existing employee representatives. Where there are no representatives, the employer must organise elections to enable employees to elect appropriate representatives. Such elections and ballots include;

---

[1] Non-Union Representation in the Workplace [2009]

- ✓ Transfer of Undertakings (Protection of Employment) Regulations

- ✓ Information and Consultation of Employees (ICE)

- ✓ Collective Redundancy Consultations

- ✓ Pre-Existing Agreement (PEA) ballot

- ✓ Joint Consultative Committee (JCC)

- ✓ Occupational and Personal Pension Schemes (Consultation by

- ✓ Employers and Miscellaneous Amendment) Regulations (PSC)

- ✓ European Works Council (EWC) and Special Negotiating Body (SNB)

- ✓ Health and Safety (Consultation with Employees) Regulations

It is usually your employer's duty to make sure that a properly conducted election takes place, which complies with all the relevant regulations. Elections are administratively demanding. The legal requirement for your employer to facilitate the elections may raise questions about impartiality since your employer is effectively an interested party in the ballot.

The role of the Employee Representative in a workplace without a recognized trade union is particularly important since they are the only means by which employees can have a say in company decisions that affect them. Employee Representatives are also able to accompany colleagues at disciplinary and grievance proceedings.

It can be a very rewarding role in terms of your professional development, and confidence. This book aims to simplify the Law and Codes of Practice so that you are able to apply them effectively at work. Also included are templates, checklists, sample agreements and further resources to help you in your work as a non-union Employee Representative.

RESOURCES

<u>ACAS:</u>

Non-Union Representation in the workplace
http://www.acas.org.uk/media/pdf/r/p/Acas_guide_Non-Union_Representation-accessible-version-July-2011.pdf

Employee Communications and Consultation
http://www.acas.org.uk/media/pdf/i/g/Employee-communications-and-consultation.pdf

Representation at work - http://www.acas.org.uk/media/pdf/h/o/Representation-at-work-advisory-booklet.pdf

Employee Representation in the workplace: Changes and Challenges
http://www.acas.org.uk/media/pdf/n/t/Acas_Employment_relations_matters_Issue_10.pdf

Voice and Participation in the modern workplace: Challenges and prospects
http://www.acas.org.uk/media/pdf/g/7/Voice_and_Participation_in_the_Modern_Workplace_challenges_and_prospects.pdf

2 DUTIES AND RESPONSIBILITIES

Information and consultation duties are legislated for, but there are many duties that you can carry out as an employee representative with the agreement of your employer and the endorsement of your colleagues. There are many jurisdictions governing individual employment rights, from unfair dismissal to protected characteristics in discrimination. An employee representative can provide support for colleagues when problems with these rights occur.

2.1 The right to be accompanied

Every employee has the right to be accompanied to a disciplinary or grievance hearing by virtue of **Section 10 Employment Relations Act 1999** and the **ACAS Code of Practice on Discipline and Grievance Procedures**. Note that this is a right to be accompanied, and not a <u>right to be represented.</u>

The right to be accompanied is a statutory right which cannot be waived by any express or implied term of contract. Your employer has to agree to any companion as long as the companion falls into one of the approved categories[2] which are,

   i. Trade union officials
   ii. Certified union representatives
   iii. Fellow workers

An Employee Representative falls into the approved category as a fellow worker. The ACAS Code recommends that the employee representative takes a full part in the disciplinary hearing.

---

[2] S10 (3) Employment Relations Act 1999

"Workers have a statutory right to be accompanied by a companion where the disciplinary meeting could result in;

- *a formal warning being issued; or*
- *the taking of some other disciplinary action such as suspension without pay, demotion, dismissal; or*
- *the confirmation of a warning or some other disciplinary action (appeal hearings)"*

The role of a companion is laid out in **S37 Employment Relations Act 2004**. A companion has the right to paid time off work to carry out the role of companion. Paid time off should cover the disciplinary hearing itself, and also allow time for the companion to update themselves about the case, and have discussions with before and after the hearing.

An employee has the right to complain to an employment tribunal if the employer denies the right to a companion[3], and the Tribunal can award compensation of up to two week's pay. Employees and workers also have the right not to be subjected to detriment for exercising their right to be accompanied. [4]

The **Trade Union and Labour Relations (Consolidation) Act 1992**[5] requires an employment tribunal to take into account any relevant ACAS Code of Practice, and permits a tribunal to increase the compensation awarded for some claims by up to 25%, where there has been an unreasonable failure by the employer to comply with a code of practice[6].

The employment tribunal would consider that an employer had not followed a fair procedure if an employee is denied the right to be accompanied at a disciplinary meeting prior to being dismissed. This would lead to a finding of automatically unfair dismissal.

RESOURCES

ACAS:

Code of Practice and Guidance on Discipline and Grievance procedures –
http://www.acas.org.uk/index.aspx?articleid=2179

Employee Rescue (www.employeerescue.co.uk):

Facing Disciplinary Action
http://www.employeerescue.co.uk/advice/i-dont-want-to-lose-my-job/im-facing-disciplinary-action/

---

[3] S11 Employment Relations Act 1999
[4] S12 Employment Relations Act 1999
[5] S207
[6] S207A

The right to be accompanied
http://www.employeerescue.co.uk/advice/i-dont-want-to-lose-my-job/right-accompanied-disciplinary-grievance-meetings/

2.2 Representation

Representation can mean anything from communicating basic information to your colleagues, through to negotiating agreements on their behalf. There is no law to allow individual representation in a non-union workplace. The only statutory right is the right to be accompanied described above.

Representation can be done with your employer's agreement, through joint consultative committees (JCCs), or "stand-alone employee representatives". Sometimes, employers can utilise existing information and consultation representatives to provide representation on grievance and disciplinary issues, harassment and discrimination.

Trade union representatives receive training from their unions and are validated to carry out the role. Employee representatives can be asked to attend employment tribunal and professional regulatory bodies as witnesses.

When acting as a companion, representatives have protection from detriment and dismissal, however the same does not apply when acting as a "stand-alone representative". To have the protection of the law, it is better to take on the representative role as an adjunct to another role in which you have statutory protection from detriment and dismissal.

For example a properly elected information and consultation representative can take on an agreed additional role as an employee representative. In such a situation the employment protections afforded to information and consultation duties would extend to the representation role.

RESOURCES

ACAS:

Representation at work - http://www.acas.org.uk/?articleid=760

Non-union representation in the workplace (Chapter 6) -
http://www.acas.org.uk/media/pdf/r/p/Acas_guide_Non-Union_Representation-accessible-version-July-2011.pdf

2.3 Negotiation

Negotiation is a tool in which dialogue is used for resolving grievances and disputes at work. Employee representatives negotiate on behalf of their colleagues during representation, consultation and even as a companion in grievance and disciplinary proceedings. It is a process by which compromise or agreement is reached while avoiding argument and dispute.

You can assist your colleagues in negotiating settlement agreements, pre-termination agreements, work as part of a team in negotiating workplace agreements or even accompany your colleagues at ACAS Early Conciliation proceedings. Negotiation impacts on every aspect of the employee representative role.

RESOURCES

ACAS:

Settlement Agreements
http://www.acas.org.uk/media/pdf/7/e/Acas-Code-of-Practice-4-on-Settlement-Agreements.pdf

Conflict Management
http://www.acas.org.uk/index.aspx?articleid=3295

Training on negotiation skills- https://obs.acas.org.uk/ViewEvent.aspx?EventId=190218

Early Conciliation - http://www.acas.org.uk/earlyconciliation

2.4 Health and Safety

The **Health and Safety (Consultation with Employees) Regulations 1996 (as amended)** require that employers allow representatives of employee safety paid time off during working hours to perform their functions. Employers must also provide training and facilities. The Health and Safety Executive says that the role of the health and safety representative is independent of management. Representatives are there to represent the interests and concerns of their colleagues and respond on their behalf. The law sets out the functions of representatives.

They represent the workforce on health and safety generally, make representations on potential hazards and dangers, attend training courses and have contact with health and safety inspectors from the Health and Safety executive or the local authority.

Only representatives appointed by trade unions can examine the causes of accidents, investigate potential hazards and dangers, inspect the workplace, and request that the employer sets up a safety committee.

RESOURCES

<u>The Health and Safety Executive (HSE):</u>

Consulting employees on Health and Safety http://www.hse.gov.uk/pubns/indg232.pdf

Training for representatives - http://www.hse.gov.uk/involvement/attendtraining.htm

Workers website - http://www.hse.gov.uk/workers/index.htm

Consulting workers on Health and Safety: Approved Code of Practice and Guidance
http://www.hse.gov.uk/pubns/books/l146.htm

2.5 Consultation

Consultation can be described as problem solving, where the employer puts forward a proposal and asks for the views and concerns of the employees and, where possible, takes these into account in making a management decision. Consultation also involves communication which is basically passing information between management and employee representatives. In **R v Gwent County Council ex parte Bryant [1988]**, the court said that fair consultation involves;

    i. consultation when the proposals are still at a formative stage;
   ii. adequate information on which to respond;
  iii. adequate time in which to respond and
  iv. conscientious consideration of the response.

There are special arrangements for negotiating consultative bodies under the **Information and Consultation of Employees Regulations 2004 (ICER),** European Works Councils under the **Transnational Information and Consultation of Employees Regulations 1999 (TICER),** European companies and European Co-operative Societies under the **European Public Limited-Liability Company Regulations 2004.**

These representatives are specially elected to negotiate and agree the design and operational rules of the consultative bodies set up under these regulations. Some may subsequently be elected to serve on the standing consultative forums.

In subject specific consultation, legislation such as the **Transfer of Undertakings (Protection of Employment) Regulations 2006**, and **Trade Union and Labour Relations (Consolidation) Act 1992 (TULRCA)** allow for the election of non-union representatives to deal with specific employment related issues such as business transfers and collective redundancy.

This also applies to pensions where the employer has a legal duty to consult with prospective and active pension scheme members and their representatives where "listed" changes are proposed.

RESOURCES

ACAS:

Employee communications and consultation -
http://www.acas.org.uk/index.aspx?articleid=675

Redundancy consultation and procedure- http://www.acas.org.uk/index.aspx?articleid=4256

3 EMPLOYEE REPRESENTATIVE FORUMS

Employers must consult with employees on the range of issues described in this book. Employers and employee representatives generally set up permanent consultative bodies for this purpose. There are many different types of consultative body and the list provided here is not exhaustive. They can be called Consultative Councils/Committees (CCs) or Joint Consultative Committees (JCCs). Some of these bodies include management and union representatives. They can consult on those issues required by law or broaden their remit to include other matters such as terms and conditions, working time, training and equal opportunities. Employees can also set up a staff association to meet with management on issues.

3.1 Joint Consultative Committees (JCC)

A Joint Consultative Committee (JCC) is used as a way of consulting employees. A JCC is made up of managers and employee representatives who come together on a regular basis to discuss matters such as working conditions, employee welfare and training.

Existing JCC's can be used in ICER processes, or new representatives can be elected onto the JCC to help inform and consult employees. To comply with ICER, existing JCC arrangements must cover all employees.

There is no particular way of selecting employee representatives for a JCC. ACAS suggests in its publication on information and consultation **Methods & Structures** that, *"employee representatives have to be genuinely representative of their constituencies. They should be directly elected by the employees they represent or should be nominated by their trade union on the basis of a member's election".*

3.2 Joint Working Groups

Joint working groups are made up of management and employee representatives who meet to address and resolve specific workplace issues together.

3.3 European Consultative Bodies

Union and non-union members of a special negotiating body, a European Company and a European Cooperative Society all have statutory rights that permit them to set up appropriate consultative bodies.

<u>European Works Council (EWC)</u>

Employees of large multinational companies based in the UK and with a presence elsewhere in Europe have a right to ask for a European Works Council (EWC) to be set up. The EWC is a body that represents employees of a multinational company in the European Economic Area (EEA) in discussions with management on transnational issues.

It brings employers and employee representatives together, in order to promote dialogue, and to ensure that employees are informed and consulted, particularly when decisions taken in another member state will affect them.

The EU Directive on establishing European Works Councils was agreed in September 1994 and implemented in the UK through the **Transnational Information and Consultation of Employee Regulations 1999 (TICER).** TICER applies to all companies located in more than one EU Member State and with at least 1,000 employees in total, of which at least 150 are located in each of two EU Member States. The right to be represented by a EWC was first introduced by the **European Works Council Directive** in 1994. This was extended to cover the UK in 1997 and was implemented in the UK through the **Transnational Information and Consultation of Employees Regulations 1999.**

A new EWC Directive was agreed in May 2009, which retained the structure and overall approach of the earlier Directive whilst introducing some important changes. The **Transnational Information and Consultation of Employees (Amendment) Regulations 2010** implements the new Directive.

European Works Councils are discussed in detail in the Employee Rescue Guide - **The Employee Representative on a European Works Council:** *A workbook on the law and processes for a non-union workplace*

Special Negotiating Body (SNB)

A EWC agreement normally follows negotiations between management and the employees. The process is triggered either by the company's management or after a written request from at least 100 employees or their representatives in two or more Member States.

Employees are represented in the negotiations by a "Special Negotiating Body" (SNB) which consists of representatives of employees from all the EEA member states in which the company has operations. The number of representatives for each member state is determined by a formula in the legislation in the State where the undertakings central management is located (or representative agent where the central management is outside the EEA).

RESOURCES

ACAS:

Information and Consultation of Employees: ICE
http://www.acas.org.uk/index.aspx?articleid=1598

Consultation - http://www.acas.org.uk/index.aspx?articleid=675

Representation - http://www.acas.org.uk/media/pdf/g/a/Acas4Representation_1.pdf

Methods and Structures - http://www.acas.org.uk/media/pdf/j/a/Acas3I_C-methods_structures.pdf

ETUC

European Trade Union Congress (ETUC) - http://www.etuc.org/

4 ELECTING REPRESENTATIVES

Employee representatives are selected through a confidential election process. In a non-union workplace, the employer must either consult with employee representatives elected for another purpose, or new representatives selected specifically for the purpose of consulting on the particular issue. Some representative roles have legally prescribed rules for elections that employers must follow. If an employer does not facilitate the proper conduct of elections, a complaint can be made to the Central Arbitration Committee and Employment Tribunal.

4.1 Selection

Some key points in elections are as follows;

- ✓ The employer must make sure that the election is fair.

- ✓ The employer is responsible for choosing the number of representatives, and must make sure that all affected staff are represented.

- ✓ The employer decides the terms of office of representatives. This should allow them

- ✓ sufficient time to complete the consultation.

- ✓ All employees are eligible for election, and no employee should be unreasonably excluded.

- ✓ Voting must be conducted in secret and the votes must be counted correctly.

- ✓ Employees should be allowed to vote for as many candidates as there are representatives to represent their class of employees.

- ✓ If no employees come forward as candidates and do not participate in collective consultation, the employer must give each employee the written information that they would have given to the employee representatives.

RESOURCES

The following organisations are authorised by the Secretary of State under employment legislation to undertake independent scrutiny and assist with running workplace elections.

Electoral Reform Services - http://www.electoralreform.co.uk/

Involvement and Participation Association - http://www.ipa-involve.com/

Popularis Limited - http://www.popularis.org/

<u>Templates (see Appendices)</u>

Sample Election Rules

Candidate Application Form

Candidate Nomination form

Letter to accompany ballot form

Voting Form

Proxy Form

4.2 Representatives of Employee Safety

The functions of non-union Employee Safety Representatives are contained in the **Health and Safety (Consultation with Employees) Regulations 1996**. Under these regulations, your employer has to consult with all employees on health and safety matters where there are no formally appointed safety representatives in the workplace. Under Regulation 4, the consultation can be done either;

  i. Directly with all employees, or
  ii. With one or more selected employees who are designated "representatives of employee safety" to distinguish them from safety representatives.

It is your employer's duty to make sure that arrangements are in place to meet these statutory requirements. Employers must decide whether to consult with employees directly or via representatives. Representatives of employee safety have the right to time off with pay for training and carrying out their duties. They are also protected from detriment[7] and from unfair dismissal[8].

RESOURCES

The Health and Safety Executive (HSE):

Consulting Employees on Health and Safety; A brief guide to the law
http://www.hse.gov.uk/pubns/indg232.pdf

Health and Safety Representatives -
http://www.hse.gov.uk/involvement/hsrepresentatives.htm

Electing Employee Safety Representatives -
http://www.hse.gov.uk/involvement/encourage.htm

Workforce elected Representatives -
http://www.hse.gov.uk/involvement/workerelectedreps.htm

Worker Involvement - http://www.hse.gov.uk/involvement/index.htm

4.3 ICER Representatives

Under the **Information and Consultation of Employees Regulations 2004 (ICER)**, employees have the right to request that their employer sets up or changes arrangements to inform and consult them about issues in the organisation for which they work and applies to organisations with 50 or more employees.

The resulting consultative bodies are sometimes called National Works Councils to distinguish them from European Works Councils.

Information and consultation representatives (ICE Reps.) are elected to negotiate a mechanism to allow information and consultation of employees called an Ice Agreement. They can also be members of the resulting consultative body. There are three types of employee representative under ICER;

---

[7] S44 of the Employment Rights Act 1996
[8] S100 of the Employment Rights Act 1996

4.3.1 Employees' Representatives

Employees' Representatives are used in pre-negotiation stages. They are not defined in ICER, however ACAS suggests that employees should be allowed to request information or challenge issues through an intermediary.

4.3.2 Negotiating Representatives

Negotiating representatives act on behalf of employees in negotiating an information and consultation agreement. There is an obligation on employers to make arrangements for employees to elect or appoint negotiating representatives in order to negotiate an ICE Agreement[9].

The election or appointment must be arranged in such a way that all employees will be represented by one or more representatives. All employees must be entitled to take part in the election or appointment process and, if there is to be a ballot, be allowed to vote[10].

An employee or an employee representative can make a complaint to the Central Arbitration Authority within 21 days of the election or appointment if any of these requirements are not met.

4.3.3 Information and Consultation Representatives

Employees have statutory rights to information and consultation under ICER. Information concerns an employer providing data to employee representatives, for example updates on significant financial and business events such as the yearly balance sheet, mergers, and takeovers as well as regular information on the progress of the company.

Consultation involves the right to be informed of planned measures in advance and to have an opportunity to express an opinion before those measures are implemented. Measures that employees must be consulted on include changes to the company's legal status, the removal, expansion or downsizing of areas of the company or business and the introduction of new technologies.

Information and consultation representatives are elected or appointed to represent employees for the purpose of receiving information from, or being consulted by, the employer.

The ICE agreement must either provide that the employer will provide information

---

[9] Regulation 14 (1) (a) ICER
[10] Regulation 14(2)

directly to, and will consult directly with, all the employees covered by the agreement or provide for the election or appointment of information and consultation representatives to whom information will be provided and with whom consultation will take place.

Where the agreement contains a provision for the election or appointment of representatives, they should be elected or appointed in accordance with that provision[11].

If there is no ICE Agreement then the Standard Provisions for an ICE agreement shall apply. This is also called the "Statutory Fall-back Provisions". These demand that information and consultation representatives should be elected by all employees and it is the employer's responsibility to organise the ballots and make sure that they are fair. This ballot must take place before the standard provisions will apply.

Regulation 19 addresses the election of information and consultation representatives.

A complaint can be made to the Central Arbitration Authority that an employer has failed to hold a ballot as required or has failed to comply with the requirements of **Schedule 2, ICER**[12].

ICER Representatives are entitled to reasonable paid time off during working hours for the purpose of performing their functions as representatives[13]. A representative who is refused reasonable time off or is not paid for it may complain to an employment tribunal[14].

Dismissal of an ICER Representative, or someone who is a candidate in an election to become one, will be automatically unfair if the reason or principal reason for dismissal is connected with their representative functions[15]. ICER representatives also have a right not to be subjected to detriment[16] and unfair dismissal and can make a complaint to an Employment Tribunal if this happens[17].

---

[11] Regulation 16 (1)(f)
[12] Requirements for ballots held under Regulation 19
[13] Regulations 27 and 28
[14] Regulation 29
[15] Regulation 30
[16] Regulation 32
[17] Regulation 33

RESOURCES

ACAS:

Employee Representation -
http://www.acas.org.uk/media/pdf/g/a/Acas4Representation_1.pdf

Non-union Representation in the workplace -
http://www.acas.org.uk/media/pdf/r/p/Acas_guide_Non-Union_Representation-accessible-version-July-2011.pdf

4.4 Pension Representatives

Pension representatives are workplace representatives who are elected for consultation over changes to pension arrangements. Your employer has a legal duty to consult with prospective and active pension scheme members and their representatives where "listed" changes are proposed[18].

The PSC Regulations apply to companies with 50 or more employees, that offer occupational pension schemes or personal pension schemes where the employer makes contributions.

Listed changes include proposals to;

- ✓ increase the normal pension age

- ✓ close the scheme to new members

- ✓ stop or reduce members' future benefit accrual

- ✓ remove the employer's liability to make employer contributions

- ✓ introduce member contributions when no such contributions were previously payable or increase them

- ✓ cease or reduce employer contributions to money purchase schemes

- ✓ change defined benefits schemes to money purchase schemes

---

[18] Occupational and Personal Pension Schemes (Consultation by Employers and Miscellaneous Amendment) Regulations 2006 (PSC Regulations)

Your employer must consult with the representatives of affected members. Where affected members are not represented either by existing union officials or ICER Representatives, new representatives must be selected. Pension representatives are entitled to paid time off to carry out their duties, and are protected from unfair dismissal or detriment.

Pension Consultation is discussed in detail in the Employee Rescue Guide - **The Employee Representative in Pensions Consultation:** *A workbook on the law and processes for a non-union workplace*

RESOURCES

Department for Works and Pensions (DWP):

Guidance on the Occupational and Personal Pension Schemes (Consultation by Employers and Miscellaneous Amendment) Regulations 2006, and the Occupational Pension Schemes (Consultation by Employers) (Modification for Multi-employer Schemes) Regulations 2006 - http://webarchive.nationalarchives.gov.uk/20130128102031/http:/www.dwp.gov.uk/docs/occ-personal-pens-schemes-regs06.pdf

Trade Union Congress (TUC):

Pensions: Practical Advice for Reps. - http://www.tuc.org.uk/pensions-and-retirement/pensions-practical-advice-reps

4.5 TUPE Representatives

Under the **Transfer of Undertakings (Protection of Employment) Regulations 2006 (TUPE),** in a situation where there are no trade unions recognised for collective bargaining purposes non-union employee representatives must be elected for the purposes of information and consultation on the transfer of undertakings and any measures proposed.

Where affected employees are not represented by a recognised trade union, the employer must inform and consult other appropriate representatives of those employees. These may be either existing representatives, or new ones elected specially for this purpose. The rules governing such an election are the same as those for a collective redundancy situation.

TUPE Representatives are entitled to paid time off to carry out their duties and for training. In addition, they are entitled to facilities to help them perform their duties as well as protection from unfair dismissal and detriment.

TUPE Representatives are discussed in detail in the Employee Rescue Guide - **The Employee Representative in a Transfer of Undertaking (TUPE):** *A workbook on the law and processes for a non-union workplace*

RESOURCES

Department for Business Innovation and Skills (BIS):

Employment Rights on a transfer of undertaking -
https://www.gov.uk/government/uploads/system/uploads/attachment_data/file/275252/bis-14-502-employment-rights-on-the-transfer-of-an-undertaking.pdf

UK Government Website (GOV.UK):

Business Transfers, Takeovers and TUPE - https://www.gov.uk/transfers-takeovers/consulting-and-informing

4.6 Collective Redundancy Representatives

Where an employer is proposing to make a number of employees redundant, at one establishment, the collective consultation provisions of the **Trade Union and Labour Relations (Consolidation) Act 1992 (TULRCA)** will apply[19]. Election rules are in **Section 188(A)** which provides compulsory timescales for consultation as follows;

i. Less than 20 employees - No compulsory time scales for collective consultation.

ii. Between 20 and 99 employees - At least 30 days consultation.

iii. Over 100 employees - At least 45 days consultation.

Your employer must consult with the appropriate representatives of any of the employees who may be affected by the proposed dismissals or may be affected by measures taken in connection with those dismissals.

Where there is no recognised trade union, or elected employee representatives, new representatives must be elected by the affected employees for the purposes of information and consultation on collective redundancies. There are two categories of employee

---

[19] S 188

representative in collective redundancies;

i. Existing Representatives

These are representatives who are experienced in the current information-gathering and consultation arrangements.

ii. Specially-Elected Representatives

These are representatives who are elected specially for the current consultation.

Your employer must facilitate the election of representatives in time for the consultation process to be completed before issuing redundancy notices. Representatives are entitled to paid time-off to perform their duties or stand as a candidate for office[20]. They are protected from detriment[21] and unfair dismissal[22].

RESOURCES

ACAS:

Code of Practice on Collective Redundancies -
http://www.acas.org.uk/index.aspx?articleid=4299

GOV.UK:

Redundancy consultation; your rights - https://www.gov.uk/redundant-your-rights/consultation

4.7 Workforce Agreement Representatives

A workforce agreement is an agreement between an employer and its employees or workers recording negotiated variations to certain statutory rights and entitlements. It is used where terms and conditions of employment are not covered by a collective agreement.

Workforce agreements cover matters such as Working Time, Maternity and Parental rights, and fixed-term employees.

If there are no pre-existing representatives in place, your employer must arrange the election of employee representatives to negotiate the workforce agreement.

---

[20] S61 Employment Rights Act 1996
[21] S44 Employment Rights Act 1996
[22] S100 Employment Rights Act 1996

A workforce agreement must:

i. be for a fixed term of not more than five years;

ii. cover all the relevant employees (or workers for the purposes of the Working Time Regulations 1998;

iii. be signed by the duly elected representatives of the employees or workers concerned or, where there are 20 or fewer employees, by a majority of them;

Copies of the text must be provided to all the employees concerned with an explanation of its meaning before the agreement itself is made available for signing. Workforce agreement representatives do not have the right to paid time off to carry out activities or for training, but they are protected from dismissal and detriment.

5 THE INFORMATION AND CONSULTATION OF EMPLOYEES REGULATIONS 2004

The **Information and Consultation of Employees Regulations 2004 (ICER)** requires UK employers to provide information to their employees and to consult with them about the operation of their business. The duty to inform and consult arises in specific situations including business transfers and collective redundancies. Other obligations to inform and consult arise for larger transnational organisations under the **European Public Limited-Liability Company Regulations 2004,** and the **Transnational Information and Consultation of Employees Regulations 1999.**

5.1 When does ICER apply?

ICER broadens the situations where businesses have to inform and consult employees. The Regulations apply to companies with at least 50 employees and whose registered office, head office or principal place of business is in Great Britain (excluding Northern Ireland) but which employ a specified minimum number of employees in the UK (including Northern Ireland). Companies are called "undertakings" in the Regulations.

An undertaking is *a public or private undertaking carrying out an economic activity, whether or not operating for gain.* A government department or local authority exercising their public functions is not an undertaking[23].

As an employee, you have rights to information and consultation if you work for a company or organisation with more than 50 employees. **Regulation 4** provides the method for calculating the number of employees. Where the number of employees fluctuates, it is calculated as an average over the last 12 months.

---

[23] Regulation 3

Non-union employees must be consulted directly or may elect employee representatives to consult with the employer on their behalf. Employee representatives must be consulted on;

- ✓ Collective redundancies
- ✓ Where part or all of a business is being sold.
- ✓ Pensions – members of occupational pension schemes must be consulted on the selection and appointment of trustees, and the trustees must keep employee representatives informed of certain information on the scheme.
- ✓ Health and safety.
- ✓ Working time.

The agreement to inform and consult is called an ICE Agreement. ICER provides two ways for information and consultation to take place in non-unionized workplaces;

i. Your employer can voluntarily start negotiations for an ICE Agreement[24], or

ii. 10% of employees in your workplace (subject to a minimum of 15 and maximum of 2500) can submit a written request for an ICE Agreement[25]

Your employer must make arrangements for all staff to take part in electing your representatives to negotiate the new ICE Agreement. These mechanisms are discussed in detail in the following chapters, together with the protections afforded by law.

5.2 Data Requests

Employees' representatives have the right to request data from their employer to find out the number of people it employs in the UK, and whether ICER applies. If the employer does not comply with a valid request for data within one month of the request, a claim can be presented to the Central Arbitration Committee[26].

5.3 Employee Request to Negotiate an Information and Consultation Agreement

The duty to inform and consult arises where the process is initiated either by employees or the employer.

---

[24] ICER Regulation 11
[25] ICER Regulation 14(3)

[26] ICER Regulation 5

You can initiate the process by making a written request that your employer negotiate an agreement for information and consultation[27]. The request must be made by at least 10% of employees (subject to a minimum of 15 and a maximum of 2,500) although a number of separate requests may be added together to reach 10% if the requests are all made within a period of six months.

You must make the request to your employer in writing, to be sent to the registered or head office or principal place of business of your employer and include the names and signatures of all employees requesting the arrangements and give the date on which it was sent.

If you want to remain anonymous you can send your request to the Central Arbitration Committee (CAC) who will make the request on your behalf. The CAC will notify your employer that a request has been made, and ask for information to verify the numbers of employees in the company, and ensure that the correct number of employees have made the request.

Your employer must acknowledge the request and tell all employees what arrangements will be put in place to negotiate an agreement on information and consultation. You and your colleagues must then elect or appoint negotiating representatives.

5.4 Employer Request to Negotiate an Information and Consultation Agreement

Your employer can also initiate negotiations by giving notice under **Regulation 11**. The notice must;

   i. be in writing
   ii. state that the employer intends to start the negotiating process
   iii. state that the notification is being given for the purposes of the ICER
   iv. give the date on which it is issued
   v. be published in such a way that it will, so far as reasonably practicable, be brought to the attention of all employees

Where one or more employers wishes to initiate negotiations to cover employees in more than one undertaking, an employer notification must be issued for each undertaking.

5.4.1 Invalid requests and notifications

Disputes about the validity of an employee request or an employer notification can be referred to the Central Arbitration Committee within one month of the relevant request or

---

[27] ICER Regulation 7

notification. An employee request or employer notification is not valid if it is made within 3 years of;

    i. the date of conclusion of any agreement negotiated under ICER
    ii. the date when, in the absence of a negotiated agreement, the standard information and consultation provisions began to apply
    iii. the date of a previous employee request where it has been followed by a ballot endorsing a pre-existing agreement

This provision will not apply if there is a material change in the employer's undertaking so that a negotiated agreement no longer covers all employees, or a pre-existing agreement can no longer be said to have been approved by all the employees.

5.5 Negotiating Employee Information and Consultation Rights

ICER makes a distinction between where there are pre-existing information and consultation agreements and where there are not.

5.5.1 Where there is a Pre-Existing Agreement

Pre-existing agreements may have been agreed between an employer and a union which is already recognised to represent staff, or where there is a Works Council or other type of staff forum already in place. Your employer cannot impose a pre-existing agreement, it must have been agreed between the employer and a union, employee representatives or the workforce.

The request to introduce new information and consultation arrangements must still be made by at least 10% of employees. If the request is made by more than 40% of employees, your employer has to start negotiations.

If the employee request for negotiations has been made by fewer than 40% of employees, then your employer may has to hold a secret ballot of all employees to determine whether they support the request to negotiate a new agreement[28].

Holding a Secret Ballot - Regulation 9

If your employer opts to organise a ballot then,

    i. All employees must be informed in writing within one month of the date of the employee request that a ballot is to be undertaken under ICER.

---

[28] ICER Regulation 8

ii. Your employer must arrange for the ballot to be held as soon as practicable but at least 21 days after employees were informed that a ballot was to take place.
iii. Your employer must make sure that the ballot is fair.
iv. All employees are entitled to vote.
v. Employees must be allowed to vote in secret if they wish.
vi. Votes must be counted correctly.

After the ballot, your employer must;

i. Notify all employees of the result as soon as possible.
ii. If the majority or those voting and at least 40% of total employees vote in favour of endorsement, your employer must initiate negotiations with a view to reaching a new agreement
iii. If the employee request is not endorsed the pre-existing agreement will remain in force.

5.5.2 Where there is no Pre-Existing Agreement

Here, your employer can start negotiations on information and consultation themselves. **Regulation 14** sets out the formalities for your employer to make arrangements for employees to elect or appoint ICER negotiating representatives. Once negotiating representatives have been elected **Regulation 21** imposes a specific obligation on both employer and employees to work in a spirit of cooperation; *"The parties are under a duty, when negotiating or implementing a negotiated agreement or when implementing the standard information and consultation provisions, to work in a spirit of co-operation and with due regard for their reciprocal rights and obligations, taking into account the interests of both the undertaking and the employees".*

5.5.3 Time Limits for Negotiation

There is a strict time limit for negotiations. Negotiations may last for six months starting at the end of the period of three months from the date of a valid employee request or employer notification. The time limit can be extended by agreement. There are also various exceptions.

5.5.4 Detail of the Negotiated Agreement

The detail of the negotiated agreement is left to you and your employer to agree. However, the standard information and consultation provisions (see below) provides a baseline for some terms that could be included. **Regulation 16** has specific requirements for negotiated agreements. The negotiated agreement must[29];

---

[29] ICER Regulations 14(3)-(5)

i. cover all employees of the undertaking although it may be made up of different parts each of which covers part of the workforce

ii. set out the circumstances in which the employer must inform and consult the workforce

iii. be in writing and dated

iv. be approved by the workforce in accordance with the provisions of ICER

v. be signed by or on behalf of the employer

vi. provide either for the appointment or election of information and consultation representatives to whom information will be provided and with whom the employer will consult, or state that information will be provided directly to, and consultation undertaken directly with, the employees themselves

vii. state that where an employer is to provide information about the employment situation, under that agreement or under any part, such information shall include suitable information relating to the use of agency workers (if any) in that undertaking. Suitable information relating to the use of agency workers' means information about the number of agency workers working for the employer, parts of the company in which they work, and the type of work they are doing.

5.5.5 Employee Approval of the Negotiated Agreement – Approval Ballot

A negotiated agreement is deemed to be approved by employees if;

i. it has been signed by all the relevant negotiating representatives, or

ii. it has been signed by a majority of the negotiating representatives and either approved in writing by at least 50% of the employees or approved by a ballot of those employees in which at least 50% of those voting voted in favour of approval[30]

ICER sets out various requirements for an approval ballot. Any claim that a ballot has not met those requirements can be made to the Central Arbitration Committee within 21 days of the ballot.

5.6 The Standard Information and Consultation Provisions (SICP)

If you and your employer are not able to reach agreement, then the SICP's will automatically apply[31]. If negotiations have taken place but agreement has not been reached, the standard provisions will apply six months after the end of the negotiation period. Where negotiations should have taken place but did not, the standard provisions will apply six months from the date on which they should have started.

---

[30] Regulations 16 and 17

[31] Regulation 20

The requirements for the SICP's are contained in **ICER Regulation 20**. Here, your employer must hold a ballot of employees to elect information and consultation representatives.

You and your employer can agree other provisions outside of the SICP's, but these will only be valid if they comply with the requirements for negotiated agreements. Employee approval can be obtained if the majority of the information and consultation representatives sign the agreement[32].

5.7 Confidential Information

Your employer does not have to disclose information if the disclosure would could be detrimental to the company. Anyone who receives confidential information from the employer under ICER obligations must hold it in confidence. If you disclose confidential information you would be in breach of statutory duty unless it is allowed by the employer or you were making a protected disclosure under **S43A Employment Rights Act 1996**. Any dispute about confidential information may be referred to the Central Arbitration Committee.[33]

5.8 Complaining

You can complain to the Central Arbitration Committee if your employer fails to comply with the requirements of a negotiated agreement or the standard information and consultation provisions. The claim must be presented within three months of the alleged infringement. This is in addition to the right to refer disputes to the Central Arbitration Committee[34].

RESOURCES

ACAS:

Reaching Agreement under the ICE Regulations -
http://www.acas.org.uk/CHttpHandler.ashx?id=118&p=0

---

[32] ICER Regulation 18 and 19
[33] ICER Part VII

[34] ICER Regulation 22

Joint Consultative Committees under the Information and Consultation of Employees Regulations: A WERS analysis – http://www.acas.org.uk/media/pdf/3/c/0414-Joint-consultative-committees-under-the-Information-and-Consultation-of-Employees-Regulations-A.pdf

6 FACILITY TIME, FACILITIES AND TRAINING

The different roles have varying rights to paid time off, training and facilities to help them in their work. The different types of statutory rights to time off, training and facilities can be confusing. To illustrate, an employee representative carrying out TUPE or collective redundancy consultation has to have paid time off, training and facilities. However, an ICER employee representative only has a right to time off, although they could be the same person carrying out TUPE consultation.

It is important to understand that the rights come with the role. All properly appointed representatives are protected from dismissal or detriment in carrying out their duties or in standing for elections. Representatives in employee forums which have been set up voluntarily by the employer have no legal rights to time off to carry out their duties, to receive training or have access to facilities. The table below sets out the statutory rights applicable to the different employee representative roles.

6.1 Facility Time

Some employee representatives have statutory rights to paid time off to carry out their duties. This is called "Facility Time". ACAS[35] advises that employee representatives should be given the necessary time off to carry out their work. Where there are no formal arrangements, it is important to get the prior permission of your employer before you carry out any work. It is important though that you have a formal arrangement with your employer. This is called a "Facility Agreement" and is discussed at **6.4** below.

---

[35] ACAS – Non-union representation the workplace (Chapter 20)

6.2 Training

The statutory framework covering paid time off for employee representatives to undertake training is inconsistent. Employee safety, TUPE and collective redundancy representatives have a legal right to training but most non-union representatives do not.

This book provides you with all the resources you need as an Employee Representative, and there are extensive free resources on the website **www.employeerescue.co.uk**., however there is some workplace specific training that you should try and arrange with your employer. These are explained in detail in the ACAS Guide and includes induction training covering areas such as;

- ✓ What your employer expects of your role as a workplace representative.
- ✓ Explanation of how time-off agreements and procedures work.
- ✓ How to communicate with your colleagues before and after management meetings.
- ✓ How confidential information should be handled.

6.3 Facilities

Facilities are the tools to help with the work of the employee representative. They include things like accommodation for meetings, access to a telephone, email and internet, dedicated office space, secretarial assistance, computers, photocopier etc.

Only Collective Redundancy, TUPE and Employee Safety representatives have a statutory right to facilities. ACAS recommends that when using facilities provided by the employer, employee representatives must comply with applicable procedures both in respect of the use of such facilities and also in respect of access to and use of company information.

The applicable procedures can be agreed between employee representatives and the employer as part of a Facility Time Agreement.

6.4 Negotiating a Facility Agreement

It is a good idea to agree time off, training and facilities arrangements in a Facility Agreement or Protocol. The agreement should be in writing with the operational date established and signed by a nominated senior manager and the representatives who were involved in drawing up the agreement. ACAS recommends that the agreement should include the following points;

✓ The number of representatives including any specialist representatives and methods of election.
✓ What time off and access to facilities is reasonable and appropriate in the particular circumstances (i.e. the circumstances where it is necessary to leave normal paid work to attend meetings with management including regular meetings of consultative bodies and the frequency with which they are held, the need for special time off to attend ad hoc meetings, grievance and disciplinary meetings)
✓ Periodic joint review of the agreement.

RESOURCES

ACAS:

Non-union Representation in the Workplace (Chapter 20) -
http://www.acas.org.uk/media/pdf/6/r/Non-union-representation-in-the-workplace-advisory-booklet.pdf

Employee Representation -
http://www.acas.org.uk/media/pdf/g/a/Acas4Representation_1.pdf

Employee Representative Statutory Rights Table

Employee Representative	Statutory Rights				
	Facility Time	Paid Facility Time	Paid Time Off for Training	Protection from Dismissal & Detriment	Facilities
Collective Redundancy	Yes	Yes	Yes	Yes	Yes
TUPE	Yes	Yes	Yes	Yes	Yes
Employee Safety	Yes	Yes	Yes	Yes	Yes
Workforce Agreement	*No*	*No*	*No*	Yes	*No*
Information and Consultation	Yes	Yes	*No*	Yes	*No*
Transnational Information and Consultation	Yes	Yes	*No*	Yes	*No*
Pension	Yes	Yes	*No*	Yes	*No*
European Company/European Cooperative Society	Yes	Yes	*No*	Yes	*No*

7 THE CENTRAL ARBITRATION COMMITTEE

The Central Arbitration Committee (CAC) is an independent arbitration body established under S259 of the Trade Union and Labour Relations (Consolidation) Act 1992. The CAC has a number of statutory functions including;

    i. Trade union recognition and de-recognition.
    ii. Voluntary arbitration of trade disputes.
    iii. Unilateral arbitration
    iv. Complaints and applications about the consultation requirements of ICER.
    v. Complaints and applications about European Works Councils
    vi. Complaints and applications about European Public Limited-liability Companies

7.1 Complaining to the CAC

The CAC receives complaints and applications about employer's obligations under ICER. With the exception of an agreement to stop court proceedings which have already started, Employee Representatives cannot contract out of the right to complain to CAC or the Employment Appeal Tribunal (EAT). Any such agreement would be void and unenforceable[36]. You and your employer can make the following types of complaints and applications to the CAC;

    i. Failure to provide data

        A complaint by an employee, or an employees' representative, that the employer has failed to provide data about the number of employees

---

[36] ICER Regulation 39

employed in the undertaking, or that the employer has provided false or incomplete data[37].

ii. <u>Ballot for endorsement of employee request</u>

A complaint by an employee, or an employees' representative, that one of the requirements for entitlement to hold a ballot or combined ballot for the endorsement of an employee request has not been satisfied[38].

A complaint by an employee, or an employees' representative, that one of the requirements relating to the arrangements for holding such a ballot or combined ballot has not been satisfied[39].

iii. <u>Employee request, employer notification/whether the obligation in regulation 7(1) applies</u>

An application by an employer for a declaration as to whether a valid employee request has been made[40].

An application by an employee, or an employees' representative, for a declaration as to whether an employer notification was valid[41].

iv. <u>Election or appointment of negotiating representatives</u>

A complaint by an employee, or an employees' representative, that one of the requirements for the appointment or election of negotiating representatives has not been complied with[42].

v. <u>Ballot for employee approval of negotiated agreement</u>

A complaint by a negotiating representative that one of the requirements for arranging   a ballot for the approval of a negotiated agreement has not been satisfied[43].

---

[37] ICER Regulation 6(1)
[38] ICER Regulation 10(1)
[39] ICER Regulation 10(2)
[40] ICER Regulation 13(1)
[41] ICER Regulation 13(2)
[42] ICER Regulation 15(1)
[43] ICER Regulation 17(1)

vi. <u>The operation of a negotiated agreement or the standard information and consultation provisions (SICP)</u>

A complaint by a relevant applicant (an information and consultation representative or, where no such representatives have been elected or appointed, an employee or employees' representative) that an employer has failed to comply with the terms of a negotiated agreement, or one or more of the standard information and consultation provisions[44].

vii. <u>Breach of statutory duty - Confidentiality</u>

An application, by a recipient of confidential information from an employer, for a declaration as to whether it was reasonable for the employer to require the information to be held in confidence[45].

viii. <u>Withholding of information by the employer</u>

An application by an employer, or an information and consultation representative, or, where there are no such representatives, an employee or an employees' representative, for a declaration as to whether the employer was entitled to withhold information[46].

ix. <u>Complaint about defective ballot</u>

A complaint by an employee, or an employees' representative, that the arrangements for a ballot for the election of information and consultation representatives are defective[47].

7.2 Proceedings of the Central Arbitration Committee

Any complaint or application to the CAC under ICER must be in writing, and in such form as the CAC may require. It must also be made within the time limit specified in the provision giving rise to the particular complaint or application[48].

A declaration or order made by the CAC must be in writing, and must state the reasons for the CAC's findings.

---

[44] ICER Regulation 22(1)
[45] ICER Regulation 25(6)
[46] ICER Regulation 26(2)
[47] ICER Schedule 2 paragraph 3
[48] ICER Regulation 35(1)

Where your employer has its registered office, head office, or principal place of business in England and Wales, any declaration or order made by the CAC may be relied on as if it were made by the High Court, and if the relevant office of the employer is in Scotland, any declaration or order may be relied on as if it were made by the Scottish Court of Session[49].

Referral to the Employment Appeal Tribunal

Where there is a question of law arising from any declaration or order of the CAC, or there is a question of law arising in any proceedings before the CAC, that matter must be appealed to the Employment Appeal Tribunal[50].

Referral to ACAS

When the CAC receives a complaint or application, it can decide that the matter can be settled by conciliation or other dispute resolution assistance from ACAS and refer the matter to ACAS[51].

7.3 Complaints and Applications about EWCs

The CAC has the power to hear and determine complaints and applications relating to European Works Councils under the **Transnational Information and Consultation of Employees Regulations 1999 (as amended).**

7.4 Complaints and Applications about European PLCs

The CAC has the power to make decisions about complaints and applications under the European Public Limited-Liability Company Regulations 2004. This is similar to its powers in respect of applications and complaints under ICER and TICER.

---

[49] ICER Regulation 35(4), (5)
[50] ICER Regulation 35(6)
[51] ICER Regulation 38(1)

RESOURCES

Central Arbitration Committee (CAC):

A Guide for Employers and Employees on the role of CAC -

https://www.gov.uk/government/publications/the-information-and-consultation-of-employees-regulations-2004-cac-publications

Issues under ICER on which an application or complaint can be made -

https://www.gov.uk/government/publications/the-information-and-consultation-of-employees-regulations-2004-cac-publications

Complain about a defective ballot -

https://www.gov.uk/government/publications/electing-information-and-consultation-representatives-make-a-complaint

Complain that a ballot has not been arranged -

https://www.gov.uk/government/publications/electing-information-and-consultation-representatives-make-a-complaint

Applications and Complaints -

https://www.gov.uk/government/collections/information-and-consultation-application-and-response-forms

APPENDICES

Sample Election Rules

1. Introduction

These rules will regulate the election of employee representatives for [*state the purpose of election*]. The rules are intended to provide clarity and structure to the election and help to ensure that the election is fair. They set down principles but do not create contractual rights and may be varied by agreement with employee representatives.

2. Appointment of election organiser

2.1 [*name and contact details*] is appointed as Election Organiser.

2.2 The role of the Election Organiser will be to ensure that the election is run fairly and in accordance with these rules.

2.3 Any employee with questions or complaints about the election should raise these with the Election Organiser.

2.4 The Election Organiser's decision on any matter relating to these rules will be final.

2.5 Unless the Employer and the Election Organiser agree otherwise, any failure to follow these rules will not invalidate an election.

3. Nominations

3.1 The employer requires employee representatives to represent employees for [*term of office for representatives*].

3.2 The employer will seek candidate nominations for the following employee representative positions: [*details of voting groups, and number of representatives required for each group*].

3.3 To be eligible as candidates, employees must have completed their probationary period, and be employed in the voting group for which they wish to be nominated as a candidate.

3.4 Employees who wish to stand as candidates must complete a candidate nomination form and return it to the Election Organiser to be received by [*date*]. Nominations received after this date will not be considered.

3.5 The Election Organiser may reject any nominations which are not correctly completed or which relate to candidates who fail to meet the qualifying conditions.

3.6 After the date for returning nominations has passed the Election Organiser will publish a list of candidates for the election and circulate this either on staff notice boards or by copying it to individuals.

3.7 If insufficient nominations have been received for one or more voting groups, the Election Organiser will make an announcement and may;

> 3.7.1. For collective redundancies and transfers of undertakings, cancel the election and give the required information to each affected employee.

> 3.7.2. Extend the deadline for receiving nominations by up to [enter number of days] working days and notify all employees.

4. Election Address

4.1 Each candidate will be entitled to produce an election address which may include one passport-size photograph of the candidate and no more than [enter maximum number of words] words of text.

4.2 The candidate will give the election address to the Election Organiser who will distribute it among the employees or place on notice boards as the Election Organiser sees fit.

4.3 A candidate may not circulate his or her election address or any other material relevant to the election or his or her nomination or both without the prior written approval of the Election Organiser.

4.4 An election address must not contain any information of a derogatory nature about any other candidate in the election.

5. Voting

5.1 The election will be conducted on the basis of first past the post.

5.2 The vote will take place on [date] from [time] to [time] at [place].

5.3 Votes may be cast either before or after normal working hours or during a permitted rest break. Votes may be cast during normal working hours only with the prior approval of the employee's line manager.

5.4 Votes are cast by returning completed voting forms in the pre-paid envelopes provided to the Election Organiser so that they are received by [insert name and title of relevant officer] no later than [date]. Votes received after this date for any reason will not be counted.

5.5 Any employee who will not be available to vote in the election, for example because of holiday or sickness, should contact the Election Organiser to arrange an advance, postal or proxy vote as appropriate.

5.6 Proxy votes may be used where the employee is absent and unavailable to vote because of holiday, sickness, maternity, adoption, paternity or parental leave.

5.7 If the employee is absent and unavailable to vote for another reason, the proxy will not be valid unless that reason is specified on the proxy form and the approval of the Election Organiser to the use of a proxy vote is obtained in advance of the election.

5.8 Employees are entitled to vote in secret.

6. Counting

6.1 The Election Organiser will take such steps as he considers necessary to ensure that the election is conducted so as to secure that the votes given at the election are accurately counted.

6.2 Candidates may be present at the counting of the votes.

6.3 The Election Organiser will announce the result of the count to the candidates present at the counting of the votes.

6.4 The Election Organiser may arrange for the votes to be recounted and if any candidate so requests [upon the announcement of the result to the candidates present at the counting of the votes OR within one hour of the announcement of the result to the candidates present at the counting of the votes] there may be one recount of all of the votes.

6.5 The Election Organiser will announce the result of any recount to the candidates present at the recounting of the votes.

7. Communicating the result to the workforce

The Election Organiser will compile a list of the winners of the election and communicate this to the workforce either by letter, email or by a written notice on staff notice boards as soon as reasonably practicable after the announcement of the results.

8. Interference with the election

Any attempt to interfere with the fairness of the election, for example by forgery of ballot papers, may result in disciplinary action by the employer up to and including dismissal.

Candidate Application Form

[Details of the voting group, for example - the whole workforce, night shift, day shift, management, non-management or department].

Candidate:	**Seconder:**
(candidate to complete)	*(seconder to complete)*
I wish to stand as a candidate for [employee] representative.	I wish to second this nomination.
Name:	**Name:**
Job title:	**Job title:**
Department/division:	**Department/division:**
Contact telephone number:	**Contact telephone number:**
Signed:	**Signed:**
Date:	**Date:**

Instructions for completing this form

If you would like to stand as a candidate for employee representative for the *[details of the voting group]* you must:

1. Complete the left hand column above.
2. Find a colleague in [insert details of voting group] to second your nomination and ask them to complete the right hand column above.
3. Return the completed form to [place/ person] by [time & date]. If the form is not received in time, you will not be able to stand as a candidate.

<u>No candidate may stand until his or her nomination has been accepted by the Election Organiser.</u>

Candidate Nomination Form

I, [*insert name*] wish to nominate [*insert name of nominee*] as an employee representative for the [*name of constituency*] constituency] at the [*insert name of office or site*].

I am employed at the above [office or site] and confirm the person nominated by me is in the same constituency as me and has consented to be a candidate.

Signed: _____

Date: _____

You must sign the nomination form to confirm that you are eligible to vote for the candidate you have nominated. This information will be treated in the strictest confidence.

Complete and return this form to [*name and job title*] by [*date*] otherwise your nomination will be invalid.

Letter to Accompany Ballot Paper

Dear [*name*],

As you know we have been receiving nominations for the election of employee representatives for [*name of constituency*] constituency

at the [*name of office or site*].

Nominations have now closed. There will be a ballot for election of employee representatives. We have enclosed a ballot paper for you to use. The ballot paper lists the people who have been nominated and who you can vote for. Details of how to complete the ballot paper, deadline for completion and delivery are also attached.

If you have any questions about the ballot, please speak to [*insert name and job title*].

Yours sincerely

[*Signature*]

Voting Form

Form No: _____

[Details of the voting group, for example - the whole workforce, night shift, day shift, management, non-management or department].

Names of candidates:

Name: **Vote:**

[insert name]

[insert name]

Instructions for completing this form

1. This is a vote to decide who you want your employee representative to be. If you do not vote you will not have a say on who your representative will be.
2. This form lists all the candidates.
3. You should vote by placing 'X' in the box next to the name of the candidate you are voting for.
4. There are [insert number] representatives to be elected. You can vote for up to [insert number] representatives. You can vote for fewer representatives if you wish.
5. If you are a candidate, you may vote for yourself.
6. Your vote will not be counted if you vote for more than [insert number] representatives.
7. Your vote may not be counted if you make additional marks on this form.
8. If you make a mistake when completing the form you must hand the spoilt form to the Election Organiser and ask for a replacement.
9. This is a secret vote. You do not have to show your completed voting form to anyone before you vote. You do not have to write your name on the voting form.
10. You should return your completed voting form by placing it in the collection box situated at [insert location] OR returning it to the Returning Officer by [date and time].
11. The vote will be counted by [insert names].
12. The election result will be posted on the notice board on [insert date].
13. If you have any questions you should contact [insert name].
14. If you have any complaints about the way in which the election is being conducted, please let [insert name] know.

Proxy Form

[*Details of the voting group, for example - the whole workforce, night shift, day shift, management, non-management or department*].

Absent voter :

(*completed by the absent voter*)

I will be absent and unable to vote personally in the election for employee representatives because of _____

I wish to appoint the person named in this form to act as my proxy and to vote as s/he thinks fit in the election.

Name:

Job title:

Department/division:

Contact telephone number:

Signed:

Date:

Reason:

Approved by:

Date:

Proxy :

(*completed by the proxy*)

I am employed in the same voting group as the absent voter named in this form.

I am willing and able to vote on behalf of the absent voter.

Name:

Job title:

Department/division:

Contact telephone number:

Signed:

Date:

Instructions for completing this form

If you are going to be absent from work and unable to vote in the election for employee representatives you may appoint a proxy to vote on your behalf. If you wish to appoint a proxy you must:

1. Complete the left column above.
2. Find a colleague from the [voting group] who is willing and able to vote on your behalf and ask him or her to complete the right column above.
3. Return the completed form to [place or person] by [time and date].

If you do not return the form in time your proxy will not be able to vote on your behalf.

NOTES

EMPLOYEE RESCUE

Employers have all the information, resources, and money. If you don't have the same resources and are not a member of a trade union, what do you have? You have Employee Rescue – http//www.employeerescue.co.uk.

Employment Law is heavily biased in favour of the well informed. Information is your friend and that's what Employee Rescue provides. We are a team of employment specialist professionals with qualifications, experience and comprehensive training in UK employment law, so that we can help you with your employment issues.

We don't operate on a "no win, no fee" basis, or provide you with any representation. What we do is provide you with the best advice on your problem on all your employment law requirements in disputes with your employer, so that you can handle it yourself or make sure that your chosen representative is giving you the right support and information.

Employee Rescue specialists provide you with all the information and support you could possibly need to make your claim. From internal procedures, ACAS Early Conciliation, Employment Tribunal, Employment Appeal Tribunal, County Court to High Court.

ABOUT THE AUTHOR

Cilinnie Ngo-Pondi (LLb.Hons) is a legal professional with over two decades experience of supporting and representing employees in the UK, New Zealand, Australia and Africa. Working with individual employees and trade unions, she has amassed a wealth of knowledge and experience of the employment problems that matter to you.